CLARENCE S. DARROW   PROF. FREDERICK STARR

Darrow-Starr
Debate

"Is the Human Race Getting Anywhere?"

Darrow - Starr Debate

"Is the Human Race Getting Anywhere?"

PROFESSOR FREDERICK STARR - YES

MR. CLARENCE S. DARROW - - - NO

Chairman: MR. ARTHUR M. LEWIS

Under the Auspices of
" THE WORKERS' UNIVERSITY SOCIETY "

Sunday Afternoon, Febuary 8, 1920, 3 O,Clock
Garrick Theatre

Chicago, Illinois

Maclaskey & Maclaskey
Shorthand Reporters
Chicago

JOHN F. HIGGINS, PRINTER AND BINDER
376-380 WEST MONROE STREET, CHICAGO

Is the Human Race Getting Anywhere?

Mr. Lewis: Professor Starr has been of very great value to this Society, and now that I have been ill and convalescing so slowly, his services here are absolutely indispensible. The Society has been the richer for listening to his lectures, and I think I have always contended, with perfect justification, that Professor Starr is the greatest living anthropologist. I don't know that science as well as he knows it, but I know it well enough to make that statement.

The subject of the afternoon, the question for debate, is, as you all know, "Is the Human Race Getting Anywhere." Professor Starr will take the affirmative of that question in a speech of twenty-five minutes, to be replied to by Mr. Darrow in a speech of forty; after which Professor Starr will have twenty, and Mr. Darrow twenty, and Professor Starr will close the debate in a speech of fifteen minutes. This is the time arranged between the two combatants. And I will now ask our good friend Professor Frederick Starr to open the discussion.

Professor Starr: I have no idea how near I shall come to observing the time arrangements that have been agreed upon. I know this, that neither Mr. Darrow nor Mr. Lewis will interrupt me, if I should overrun my time. I confess that I feel somewhat at a loss in appearing in a debate of this kind anyway, because all my training has been away from the presentation of a side, from the partisian idea. The scientific man is, through all his discipline, subjected to the idea that he must present every side with equal fullness, and it is a difficult thing indeed for me to come before you and present one side of a subject, especially a subject so interesting as this that is before us. That is what I am expected to do. I have less regret in doing so than I might have were I not sure that Mr. Darrow will find everything that is to be said on the other side. So that there is no danger that it will not be adequately presented.

I want first of all to call your attention to a rather interesting fact that bears upon this subject; I want to call your attention to the three men who have appealed to you from this platform. I want to call your attention to Mr. Lewis, first. Arthur M. Lewis is well known for his interest in astronomy. That is

his stronghold.   Astronomy is where he shines and is strong.
In his lectures on the spectrescope, the moon and the sun, nobody, I believe can outdo him.   But that is not the point.   The
point is this: Mr. Lewis' interest in astronomy, is progress, is
evolution, is development—don't you see?   He deals with
specific things, he deals with matter, but he is not interested in
dead matter.   However tenuous, however widespread, however quiescent, is it dead matter that Mr. Lewis is interested in?
No.   It is matter when it begins to move.   It is matter when it
gets to forming something.   It is an evolution that he follows.
He takes that matter that was distributed so tenuously through
space, and he follows it through its evolution in one form or
another, through the whirling nebula into some planetary form
—or the great sun, or the moon.   See what it is?   It is dynamic, and it is dynamic going somewhere, all the way through.
Notice that matter.   It is there just as much when he gets
through with that splendid evolution as it was when he began.   Just as much of it there.   Just as inert in itself, and just
as quiet, just as tenuous.   But his interest is not in the dead
matter, it is in the movement, it is in the development, it is
in that splendid series of thoughts that one gains when he
stands in the presence of those majestic, heavenly bodies,
sweeping so regularly through the heavens.   Is that progress?
Is that getting anywhere?

Now, here in the same way is Clarence Darrow.   Mr. Darrow tells us, on every possible occasion, of his deep interest
in biology.   Well now, you all know what biology is.   Biology
is the science of life.   There was some time in the history of
the universe when life appeared on this planet.   I don't know
just when; he does not know just when; no one knows just
when, nor how, nor where, life first appeared upon this earth;
but life appeared, and no doubt it came first in very simple,
very low, poor forms.   I have no doubt that we have plenty
of just such poor, simple forms yet living, in other words, unicellular.   Unicellular beings are as plenty today as they ever
were; but do you think Clarence Darrow's interest in biology
is confined to those simple forms?   Do you think that he
spends his time only in thinking of the moment and the place
and the way in which life first appeared?   Nothing of the
kind.   His interest in biology is in development, in growth, in
evolution, in the way in which the simple becomes complex;
in the way in which those poor, mean, miserable unicellular
forms came to be something.   Yes, he is interested in biology
because it is progress; because it is an evolution; because there
is a getting somewhere.   He would not be content to be interested in poor beginnings, never.

Neither am I.   I am interested in anthropology.   There

was a time in the history of the world, when man appeared upon the earth. Pretty poor kind of man he was; didn't know much about himself. Perhaps he was not even self-conscious. Probably he did not know what part he was playing. He knew some things as other animals know some things, yes; but he went forward. Of course, he went forward. Do you think I am interested in knowing only just when man began, and what poor, miserable, beginning-man was like? Why no. It is man as he evolves, man who develops, man who comes from one step to another, higher and higher until finally he belts the world with his system of transportation; he annihilated space and time; he conquers and harnesses the powers of nature. It is that evolution that interests me. I would be no more interested in focusing my attention upon the poor, miserable beginning-man than he would on unicellular forms,— or than Lewis would on dead and inert matter. No, it is the fact of progress; it is the fact of evolution; it is the fact of development; it is the fact of growing complexity out of simplicity that interests us and every man. You know it is just the same way with every man, woman and child in this building. You have all of you something that you are interested in. Of course you have, everyone of you. How glad I am that they are different things. Wouldn't it be a dreadful earth if we were all interested in one thing and nothing else? It would be unbearable, absolutely. Lewis sometimes finds fault with people who like art—I mean Darrow does; Lewis never does. Lewis never finds fault with anybody who likes anything. But Darrow sometimes pretends that he despises the man who loves art. Think of it. You know that it takes all kind of men to make a world, and the man who loves art has just as much business in life and just as much right to be here as the man who is so devoted to biology.

Now, notice this fact. Each one of you is interested in the thing that interests you as a live thing. You are interested in it because it is moving. You may think that things are pretty bad, indeed, you may be interested from the point of view of reformation; from the point of view of putting the push into things; from the point of view of elevating and helping people. That may be your object. But, whatever you are interested in, you are interested in it from the point of view of evolution, from the point of view of progress, from the point of view of getting somewhere; and you know well that there is a possibility of progress; you know well that there is a possibility of development; or else you could not ever be interested in the thing that you are interested in.

Well, that is a fundamental proposition which I think it is just as well to have laid down here at the very beginning. Now, let us make it somewhat concrete. Let me call your attention to the question, whether in this society as we know it, and in this world in which we live, there have been progress and development and there is reason to look for progress and development in the future. Many of the most important things that man ever did, many of the greatest inventions that he ever made, many of the most important discoveries that he has found, are so simple that we look back upon them as if they had always been part of our equipment.

For instance, take a single thing—take the discovery of fire, the learning of its uses, the taming of it, the employment of it in different ways, to add to man's comfort or protection or pleasure. Fire! the discovery of fire, the learning how to make fires! Why, I have a whole lecture on the subject that I do not ever expect to give here, so I am quite free to tell you it. I have a lecture on the subject of fire, and of the value of fire to mankind. Its influence in human life, its effect on society cannot be overstated.

Well now, we are so used to those great discoveries that were made by some men anciently, that were taken over into daily life, that were practiced continuously ever since, and that are still in use among us, that we forget what they mean; we forget their importance, their significance. I want you to realize that we have in our society and in our daily life, a thousand acquisitions from the distant past that were the result of men who thought and lived and acted in those older days, and I want you to realize that a really useful thing, after it has once gained use, usually stays. After they once controlled fire, after they once learned its real uses, men the world over knew how to make fire and to keep fire and to use it in one and a hundred ways.

We have in our life, many things, thousands of things that have been accumulated through the ages, through the activities of so many different, forgotten men. And, talk about our not having made any progress! Our everyday life is based on acquisitions made through the centuries and milleniums by our unnamed ancestors.

Of course, we have also many things we can put our finger on and say from whence we got them. Have we progressed? Look at our culture and see whether we have progressed. See whether we have beautiful things, valuable things, helpful things, that have come to us from one or another of the old civilizations of the past. One of the oldest, is that great culture that used to exist between the rivers in Mesopotamia. I have often thought that if I were a real young man and had my life to live over again and knew anything like what I know now, that I would go to Mesopotamia to live. It is one of the great districts of the world. They have had culture after culture in Mesopotamia. In those days, those old men were interested in measuring time; they were interested in marking out circles; they were interested in dividing circles. Sixty seconds make a minute; sixty minutes make an hour; twenty-four hours make a day; twelve signs or three hundred and sixty degrees make the circle. All this useful knowledge comes to us from Mesopotamia.

Mr. Darrow will ask you the utility of knowing all these things. But you know we could not get along without them. Don't let him fool you by asking you. I see you understand, so there is no need of my saying any more along that line. Well, now, we have that from Mesopotamia. What of our splendid means of knowing all the great thought of the past? What of the art thereof by which the present and the future will know what we are thinking—the art of writing? You know, the future would be poorer if it did not read of the splendid efforts of my opponent, at different times. We can transmit the record only because in Egypt they learned to write. From Egypt there went out the knowledge of letters, of the alphabet, the thing that has made us to know what the past has thought, the thing that carries on the thought of the present into the future. Great achievements! Even Clarence Darrow realizes that that is something. Oh, hear him talk about the beautiful thought of one writer and another! There is no man more appreciative of fine things that have been achieved than he is, only he is ashamed to say so.

There was Greece. Greece made its contribution, and that was that much despised, artistic contribution. Ah, but it was something to build such wondrous buildings as the old Greeks erected. It was something to give those splendid lines in architecture; it was something to give those ideas of pure form in decoration; it was something to give such ideals of sculpture and of painting as the old Greeks gave us. It was something to give those splendid tragedies; those wonderful theatrical and dramatic performances, all preserved to us through the medium of Egyptian letters.

And Rome? Why, yes, Rome gave us system, strength, and government and law. Why, we are the heirs of all the ages! A quotation by the way; not an original statement on my part—but, we are the heirs of all the ages, and we have the fine things that the Mesopotamians developed, that the Egyptians invented, that the Greeks created, and that Rome devised, and yet there are people who question whether there is such a thing as progress!

Well, now, if we have been the heir of all the ages, it is worth while to ask whether we have ourselves contributed anything. What have we done for the future? What contribution have we made to help the world advance? Our achievement is really an extraordinary one, and it is to a certain extent new. It is true that the civilization which has been developed during the last three hundred years, differs strikingly at least in degree from any civilization that ever preceded it in the way that it has learned to know the forces of nature and to control and direct them to useful ends.

In other words, we have been living in a period when our greatest achievement has been in the direction of the control of material forces; when our greatest attainment has been in the line of physical and material science. It has been an age of thought distinctly materialistic, blossoming into a period of absolutely mechanical invention and development of machinery. . You know how rapid that development has been. I am not an old man, but I was a well-grown boy before there was such a thing as a telephone; and not very far back of that was the telegraph. I told Mr. Darrow before we came in here that I had not engaged in a public discussion since I was seventeen years old. That is really true. And when I was seventeen years old we used to discuss such things as "Is it possible to have a horseless carriage?" We decided it was not possible. We demonstrated definitely that there were frictions and inertias and things of that kind which could not possibly be overcome. We were all satisfied. Then we debated questions about whether there was utility in baloons and the efforts to fly. We had a funny poem in those days, about a man named Green and his flying machine and his name Green was suggestive of his natural verdancy in thinking of such a thing as a flying machine. You have seen what changes have taken place; today flying has become almost a controllable thing. We have made our contributions, yes; we have made our contribution, the beauty of which some people do not see. We have made a contribution which some people feel has taken all the joy out of life. There are those that think—that materialistic science, that this inventive age, this age of mechanism, that this control of natural forces has crushed out much that was finest and best in humanity. And there are many people who do not look upon it as an unmixed blessing. But, it is a contribution, yes, it is a great contribution. And proof of it will remain, when we are gone and our names are forgotten, when we have given place to new generations; there will be something left of this marvelous period with its Edisons and Morses and other great inventors and discoverers. We will be a genuine contribution to the world. It will be in the question of helpfulness and progress, and life will be better and stronger and happier and the world will be upon the whole advanced by these things.

So I make the second point: That we, ourselves, live in a time, when all that we have is due to the ages that went before, with a little increment which we, ourselves, have added.

Now, I want to define civilization. I am not going to give you the anthropologic definition which I failed to give you last week. I received a wail last week that I did not state what it is that constitutes civilization. I meant to do it; but I did not. I am not going to give that definition today; but I am going to give you this definition:

Civilization is the adjustment of the individual to living in a crowd. You get the idea? That really is what civilization is, the adjustment of the individual to living in a crowd. And if mankind prospers, and develops biologically, and is not a failure, we have got to live in a crowd from now on. The world becomes more and more crowded, and civilization becomes more and more necessary as the adaptation of the individual to live in a crowd. In other words, do not think for a moment that civilization is a thing that is going to disappear. No, no, civilization in its true sense is a thing which must be, because the crowd is here, the crowd is coming, the world is full, it is getting fuller, and every human individual must adjust himself to that mass in which he lives or else he is crushed and dies.

That is what civilization is. That is what we must look at, for only as the individual becomes adjusted, developed, as he becomes more complex in his interests and in his contacts, that progress is made.

I want to call your attention, as of course, he will presently and I am willing to leave the details of it in his hands, because he will do it perfectly indeed, to the course of civilization in the past. I have spoken of civilizations that have existed and that have made some contribution upon which we have drawn. Now, let us see what the course of such civilizations have been.

There were those Mesopotamian civilizations. Not one, but three of them, one after the other. They grew up, splendid developments and complex; wonderful inventions, great discoveries, vast refinement, much luxury! Then, they fell, one after the other. Persia rose and fell, and Egypt rose and fell, and Greece rose and fell, and Rome rose and fell. Well, what of it? The mere fact that they fell did not set back the world. Every time that one of those great civilizations fell— that is, culminated and began to grow down hill,—there was always a population ready, some vital, vigorous, fresh, new-blooded population, to seize the falling torch and carry it on. Civilization has never disappeared from the hour it was first developed on the globe, until the present day. It has never disappeared.

Civilization once here, has simply changed its place; simply changed the population among whom it showed itself. In every case civilizations have passed on the torch to those who came after them.

I have wondered a good deal about the future in this matter of civilization. I have often wondered who was to catch the torch when this civilization should have culminated and, then should go to ruin. For I have predicted for many years that our materialistic civilization would end. I believe it firmly. I think the moment is near. I think we are living in the very crisis of the civilization that you and I have seen. I am by no means sure that we are going to get through that crisis and retain civilization.

A few years ago I felt certain that we would not, and I see very little in the present situation to assure me that we are to retain the civilization of which we have been so proud and for which we have tried to do so little.

Well, what reason do I have for doubting whether there is a future for our civilization? Do not misunderstand me. I am not arguing for Mr. Darrow. I am only getting ready for him to go on from the point where I leave off. This is a moment of crisis; this hour is the most discouraging hour that we have seen in our lifetime. This is a serious question, whether our civilization can stand or whether it must pass. Always heretofore, there has been, as I say, some fresh, vigorous, new-blooded population that could catch the torch and go on with it to even higher things. There was a time when I used to hope and believe that there might be some young nation in the far east, who would seize the torch from our hands before the blaze expired. But, the world has shrunken; the world has shrunken. This materialist victory I have spoken of is very real.

It is hard to find a population but what has the virus of our disease. I look in vain for the nation which, I hoped, might be ready to seize the dying torch, and lifting it up into a fresher oxygenated air, advance to higher things. I used to hope for such a nation. Now, you are waiting to hear Mr. Darrow, and I purposely have led up to this point. I do not think he could have a better place to begin than here.

The Chairman: That is like paving the way for the opponent. If you will watch our program, I will let you know when we are going to have that lecture on fire on this stage. Mr. Darrow will now reply.

Mr. Darrow: Professor Starr is so much like my old time friend and antagonist whom I still am mourning, Professor Foster, that it makes my side easier. He is not a lawyer; he is a college professor, and is honest. It is impossible for him to put his side of the question without pretty well putting my side too. Of course, I have an advantage. I can put my side without putting his. I am aware though, that this advantage is more than overcome by his superior learning in those things that are important in a discussion of this kind.

I am not here to discuss whether man is better and higher than the Ameba. I could not discuss that for I really do not know. Of course, man has more legs to——get the gout in and he has a bigger stomach——to be diseased, and he has a bigger brain——for the home of more false theories. Most of these questions get us back to another question, "What is it all about anyhow, and what do we mean by getting anywhere?" The Ameba has one advantage over us, if it is an advantage, the Ameba is endowed with immortal life. I am not saying that this is an advantage; neither does the Ameba have to work so hard. Whether his simple organism is better than the complex organism that is given to man, I don't know. I have to ask myself, "better for what?" Then, I am lost, as I fancy anybody else is lost. The Ameba can't construct words as man can, and he does not need them. Probably man does not either, but that is not the question. The question is, "Is the Human Race Getting Anywhere?" not whether the Ameba is or not.

If the human race is higher, which we will assume, to save trouble——then is this higher race getting anywhere, and if so, where?

I did not know that I had such an antipathy towards art. In fact, I thought I was some artist myself. I am rather fond of art; the world has lost a large part of what art it once had. We have abandoned art to make money, which to me is not a sign of progress. If I did not believe in art, I might think that steam engines were better than pictures or sculpture, but I don't think so. I suppose there is a certain value in measuring the seconds and the hours and the weeks and the years. It gives you a chance to know about when you are going to die.

Really, I am unable to say what are the valuable things in life. I used to think the main thing was to have property evenly divided. I am now uncertain about that. I used to think if we could get property evenly divided, we could get brains evenly divided. I am sure now we could not, and if we could nobody would have very much to boast of. The trouble with all these questions is to get a starting point. What is life for?

No one can answer that question. I am sure of it, because I cannot answer it myself. If we can not answer that we may then ask the question: What are we to do with life now that we have it thrust upon us, in this case we are not very much better off. My own idea is that on the whole, the life is the most tolerable which has the greatest measure of pleasurable emotions against painful ones. Some people might say that life is to gather wisdom. But, I don't know what we are to do with our wisdom. I have been gathering it all my life, and I don't know what to do with it now that I have it. Or, is it to build steam engines? What for? Suppose these produced painful emotions instead of pleasant ones? Is it to make guns? What for Or, to make flying machines, so we can use them in wars? There is no starting point. But, that never discourages me. I see in life, just what the Professor showed us in the end, a continual coming and going. One civilization or one set of ideas, taking the place of another. Nations growing civilized, as he calls it, so they can get along with each other, and then killing each other.

I see it in the Persians, creating what was a great civilization, and then in that civilization being destroyed. I see it in the Greeks, and the Romans, creating what in many ways, was a great civilization, and then going to pieces, utterly destroyed. And, generally, by what and by whom? Generally by some primitive people who are living close to the foundation of nature, close to the earth and air, and the sunlight, who have not the seeds of disease and disintegration, which a civilization plants in all human kind.

I see no beneficient power in evolution. I see no beneficent power in the universe which says that of necessity man shall get better or higher, or what to me is more important, happier. I see with human life what I see with the ocean, an everlasting ebb and flow; the flow pretty clearly marked and the ebb pretty clearly marked; marked by an inexorable nature. Nothing that man can change, and the more he tries to change it, the sooner he dies.

We all protest the cruelty of nature. And, yet, if we live, we must live the abject slave of this unfeeling monster which we call nature, she, to my mind has fixed the limits of man and fixed them absolutely.

Civilization, as the Professor says, is the faculty of living together, and he likewise says that the world is getting more crowded every day. So, sooner or later we will have to turn to and cut each others throats, because there won't be room for us, and ever since the world began we have been doing this so the more you are civilized, the more the necessity of cutting your neighbor's throat.

Assume we have reached man in animal life, and that man is the highest organism that the earth has ever known. Perhaps he is. Then, what about this "human race?" Is it getting anywhere, and if so, where? If I were to ask you the question as to whether the ants and the bees are getting anywhere, you would probably say no. The ant and the bee takes just as good care to see that its species is perpetuated as man does; and nature seems to be interested in one thing, and that is the preservation of life.

At a certain stage the ant and bee were evolved and the types became fixed. I fancy there will be no dispute about that. The ant and bee today can do nothing that their ancestors could not do, when the first ant and first bee no doubt proclaimed to each other the wonders of the ant and bee creation. They cannot get beyond their structure. It is fixed. The same thing, I take it, is true, of all other animal structures. You can develop nothing from a cow, but a cow. You may put more fat on it so it will be more desirable to eat, but you can make nothing out of it but a cow; any amount of fat that you put on is limited, because too much fat will kill it, just as it kills civilization. The species is fixed.

Nature we will say, by some mutation, produces the ape and the monkey, and when these were produced, it got through with that job. There are some monkeys that weigh more than others, and some that can chatter louder, just the same as there are some of us debaters that can talk louder and longer than others. But, the ape and monkey business is finished. I suppose that even a socialist would not care to go to the apes to teach socialism. He would think he was wasting time. The ape hasn't the stuff in him. He is finished. Assume that by a twist of evolution, that man came into being.

Is man different from the ant and bee and the cow and the ape? Of course the theologian says he is different, because the Almighty made his body and then planted in him a soul; but the scientist cannot find the soul. The doctors have dissected men, and they cannot find it; and the grocers have weighed the dead men and the living, and they cannot find it; and the evolutionist and the scientist have pretty much come to the conclusion that he was made just as the ape was made and the ant was made and is purely a natural product, in fact, a machine. Man, as I take it, is finished.

I am not saying that some day on account of a change of climate or some mysterious turn of nature, some higher spe-

cies might not appear upon the earth. I can not tell and I
never will know. Perhaps some day the superman will be
born, but if he is, he will be like the ape and the monkey and
the ant and the bee,—he will be fixed. When the superman
comes, if he does, what about the "human race?" Why, the
superman will treat the human race as horses, to be slaves, or
as hogs, to be eaten, to feed the superman. Man's stature is
fixed, according to all the laws of biology, you spoke of. According to all we know of life, according to all we know of
nature which is heartless and cruel, and has no interest in anything—except to fix the contrivance up so that life will persist.
Although you are not sure of that. In two or three different
periods in the last two hundred thousand years, the ice age has
swept down upon the earth and destroyed any amount of living species, men with the rest; not entirely, but in many locali-
ties.

Now, what is man? He has a clear history. You can tell
what man came from and how much he will come to, just as
much as you can tell what will happen to an egg if a hen sits
on it. Some hens may be bigger than others, and noisier, and
some foolisher, but they won't be much bigger, or much noiser
or much foolisher; could not be. And it has been true since
the first hen, or the first egg, whichever came first—and we
will not settle that, either.

Man has a plain history. A germ is fertilized and he is
built cell on cell, and you know how big he will be and what
size his brain will be, and about when he will die. Of course,
he may be a little bigger or a little smaller, but not very much
larger or very much smaller. The biggest brain that any intelligent person ever had, as I recall it, and I asked the Professor here, before he came on the stand, to make sure of it—
the biggest brain was sixty-four ounces. If you get up to sixty-
six it makes an idiot. So you can't get it any bigger, so far as
experience shows, and sixty-four was a mighty close shave.
Of course, you can make an idiot with a great deal smaller
brain; I have known lots of them. But, when you get above
that it is sure to be one. So, what are you going to do?

To hear some of these people talk who believe in eternal
progress—that is the eternal progress of the "human race,"
you would think that some time a man was to have a brain
as high as the Masonic Temple; but he is not, and if he did,
he must have legs, and a stomach to match, and all the rest
of the machinery to go with it, or he would be lost. He is
fixed. And he has probably been fixed for tens of thousands
of years. Not only is it impossible to change his brain but
his brain and its action depends on his stomach and lungs and
his legs, and he must keep up the balance. A man buys an

automobile and stops running and cannot digest his food, so he dies. Of course, the surgeons work on him awhile, but they cannot keep him alive forever, because he is out of balance, any more than you can keep an ape living in a cage. He is a part of nature, and he must live with her, or he dies. His brain is fixed; his whole structure is fixed, and if we can learn anything from other animal life and from life, it is impossible to change it.

Of course, he may turn his brain in one direction or another. He may go a certain distance in one direction or another, but if he goes east, he cannot go west; and if he goes north, he cannot go south; and if he takes up mechanics, he will probably lose art and the things that are the most worth while for man.

Now, I fancy that Professor Starr would have an easy time to prove that we have more railroads and taller buildings and larger cities now than there where a hundred thousand years ago, or even six thousand years ago, when perhaps the written history of the human race began. He would have an easy time to prove that so-called civilized people have more thickly inhabited cities or more mechanical devices or more money than the savages in Africa. That is easy. But he might have a very much harder time to prove that man is intrinsically stronger, and a still harder time to prove that he is happier, which to my mind, is the best measure of whether we are getting anywhere or not. Of course, the Professor is more familiar with the savage than I am. I don't say this because he has lived so long with the College Professors down at the University, but because he has traveled in Mexico and Africa and countries outside of America. Of course anybody outside of America is a savage! At least he can not be a hundred per cent American! But I could not prove that a savage in Africa was not as happy as a civilized banker in Chicago, if you can put those two words together. The savage does not have to watch the ticker to see whether stocks are going up or down; and he does not need to worry because he can't get all the money there is in the world, and he does not have to be operated on for appendicitis or anythink like that, and he knows nothing about germs.

On the question of happiness, I doubt whether civilization gets you anywhere. Of course, the African lives a sort of life close to nature, and I presume he does pretty well. I could picture the African sitting on the banks of the Congo. That isn't so bad—sitting in the shade, playing with the alligators, his children around him, and his wives out gathering bread fruit and cocoanuts for him. What's the matter with that! I fancy you couldn't improve his condition by putting up a silk mill for his children to work in or a steel mill for him to work in!

I think it is impossible to say that civilization has done anything to make life happier, or more tolerable for the everlasting stream of men and women that come and go. Is there any sense in saying that the world is getting anywhere; and if so, where? Is this generation happier than the last? A great many things have come into being in my lifetime. Of course, I am not much older than the Professor, but still I can remember when the telephones came. Now, I get sore every day by being called up every three or four minutes on the telephone. Has the telephone added to the pleasures of life?

I can't see that life is any happier now than it was when I was a youngster. I fancy the people when I was a youngster were just as happy as they are now, and perhaps happier. They were all sure they were going to heaven after they died, and most of us are not so sure now. Really, one must get a starting point, and I can't find one. Wherever you place your feet, is quick-sand. Is it intellect that makes you happier? Why, of course, I know better than that! Because I am not happy. Is it money that makes you happy? I know better than that, too. Is it tall buildings? No, my office is on the thirteenth floor. What has that got to do with it? Is it railroads? I hate to ride on the cars.

What makes happiness? Well, I fancy it is largely a state of mind and I know nothing between savagery and Christian Science that can change the state of mind. Of course, socialism may to a degree, but it is only to a degree, because the Socialists expect something here, and the others don't, so even they can be disappointed. But take any basis that we can think of. The intellect is a poor one. Can you prove that the intellect of man is any better than it was, or that it is going to be? I don't know about the Neanderthal man, who lived sixty thousand years ago; a little of his skull was found in a cave in western Europe. We hav'nt got enough to judge. But I know something about man as far back as the history of the human race goes, and our men are certainly no more intelligent today than they were then. We have'nt got beyond Plato, and Aristotle and Socrates, although we have Mary G. Baker Eddy and Dowie and Billy Sunday and Bryan!

When I was making a memorandum coming down about what I should say, the only thing I really put down was "Bryan," to prove that the world did not move." It is perfectly clear that man has not improved in twenty-five hundred years. It is true, that there have been more books written lately, but very few of them are worth reading. Anybody can write books if he has learned how to write. Everybody can speak because they have learned how to talk, but it does not show that they are saying anything, so we still go back to Plato and Aristotle and Socrates and that brilliant galaxy of philosophers and thinkers who have made up a large share of all the geniuses of the world.

Intellectually man has got nowhere. If he has, I don't know where. What has he done? Intellectually, he has done nothing. He has turned his mind to this thing and that, and he has preserved some of the things that other generations knew of, but as an intellectual machine, as a human being, he is no better. Swept onto the earth with the rest of life, born, lives his time and passes away.

Have we learned anything about war? Why everything that was said against war was said twenty-five hundred years ago, at least. The world has been educated about its cruelty for hundreds of years, and yet in the midst of our wondrous civilization, we have seen the greatest war of history, and every bit of science that we knew has been called into play for the purpose of killing men. I wrote a book on non-resistance fifteen years ago and we have had a war since that! And I believed in it myself. The primitive man, with all of his old primitive instincts, is here just the same as the first man, and these instincts rule his life.

When we come down to modern life, what have we learned? One hundred and fifty years ago we formed a nation, dedicated to freedom of speech and freedom of action, and what has become of it? Look at the great gallaxy of scientific men who have taught the world for the last two hundred years at least. Yet, the world has gone crazy over tipping tables and hearing raps on the ceiling to prove immortal life. Think of the more or less philosophical ideas of life, and the future, and religion. And you can plant in a civilization like the United States the doctrines of Dowie and Mary Baker Eddy. Think what has been done and said by all the wise of all the ages, about philosophy, and along comes a cheap evangelist like Billy Sunday and a cheap politican like Billy Bryan, and they make the people declare by law what you and I shall drink and not drink! Have we got anywhere? If we have, I wish we could go back!

America entered into a war, partly to make democracy safe in the world; we founded a nation with a constititution, which was meant to preserve liberty and a declaration of independence which came from the wisest and the freest men of their age, declaring the mind to be free and that men should be free; and we finished with the war and then a few vote-monging politicians moved by the people who love wealth and power have turned a great, free country into a mad-house! A mad-house where the human mind is paralyzed and the human lips are dumb for fear of the wrath of the money changer! We have destroyed as far as a few years' can destroy, the free institutions that it took centuries to rear; we have made a psychology that causes us to look back at Herod and the Duke of Alva and the Witch-burners and admit that they were pikers compared with us!

The Chairman: Professor Starr will continue the debate for twenty minutes.

Professor Starr: I really feared when his forty minutes were fully up, that he was going to sit down without saying anything new, and I should have been greatly disappointed if that had been the case, because you do not come and listen to him talk for forty minutes without saying anything. Of course, I think he is fixed. And, you may take it in either sense of the word you please; you may either take it from the point of view of this debate, or you may take it from his usual, intellectual attitude. But, that is neither here nor there.

I was a little astonished at some things he said. I was disappointed in some things connected with his attitude. I have heard him say so much about his vast knowledge, and I knew of his interest in biology, therefore my pain was great when he said that for himself he could not tell the difference between a man and an ape, a cow, a bee and an ant. Think of that! Think of that! I was sorry he did not ask me about something besides the weight of the brain under those circumstances, because I would have been glad to have told him the difference between a cow and an ant, for instance, before he came in. However, you know the difference between a cow and an ant. One difference between a cow and ant is that the cow is very far from being a social being; very far from being a species that has developed a high degree of culture and of society, while an ant is a socialized being. There is propriety in saying that an ant and bee is a fixed species. There is propriety in saying that they have developed to a certain point and it is very unlikely they will make any change —and probably a change would be for the worst if it could be conceived. But an ant and a bee are things that have become perfected, from the point of view of social organization.

Now, I am not sure it is a desirable thing, and I am glad that man, as yet, is not so fixed as the ant and the bee. Nothing but most thoughtless use of words could possibly lead to such a suggestion. Ants and bees are fixed socially and mentally. The organization is perfected, it cannot be changed without being damaged. He has shown that we can be changed with profit. Am I right? Has he shown that we can be changed with profit? If so, what is to prevent our profiting and making that change? Are you really automata? Are you really helpless? Didn't some men make that constitution that he has praised so highly? Did not some men make that declaration of independence? And I am certain that in the two generations that have passed, or three, since those splendid papers were written, there has been no such mental degeneration as to prevent our showing us to be worthy grandchildren of those sires.

If we are living in a mad-house, it is time we got out of the mad-house. If we have gone backward in the five years just passed, it is time for everyone of us, if we are honest, to buckle down and to say that the bad of these five years must be undone. The results of the next five years must be much better. We can do it because mankind is not yet either ant or bee, but human beings, that can work for progress!

Talk about the telephone! He said that he was a slave to the telephone. Well, now, you know, I am no slave to the telephone. There is no man, woman nor child that has ever heard my voice through that accursed machine. I might not live on the thirteenth floor of a building, but I have enough control over myself and my actions in the City of Chicago, not to do what I do not want to do! I am not fixed!

Now, you notice, I thought he was really a very free-thinker. I thought he really had broken away from the ideas of the past. I thought that if any man in this house was able to completely cut loose from this anthropo-morphising of things, it was Clarence Darrow, and yet he talked of us as being in the hands of a monster, "Nature." In the hands of a monster. Think of its claws; think of its heart; think of its hands, this monster, "Nature," and then find fault with weak minds who anthropomorphise.

You know, it pains me, because I meant to have said some nice things about Clarence Darrow, and to have to modify, even in the slightest degree the kind remarks which I had suggested in my outline, becomes painful to me. Another thing, I am surprised at the way it appealed to this audience. He said that only a few years ago, when he was a boy, everybody felt sure that they were going to heaven, and then he spoke of the awful come-down to the present time, when people are not so sure. Now, you know, what could he have found so delightful in the picture of eternally thrumming on the harp; yet he seems to think that is a come-down! Notice, notice, such inconsistency! And to a man who is fixed. You know, I knew I should have to say something to overcome the effect of his foolery. So, at this point

I have said this to meet his quibs and jokes! Well, he will
have a new stock of them later on, but they will be no worse
than the ones he has given.

Now, dear friends, I referred at the close of my introduc-
tion to the dreadful situation in which we are. Mr. Darrow
cannot paint the situation worse than it really is. There is
chaos throughout the world. I know it; every thoughtful man
knows it; everybody but those who blindly swear by those old
men at Paris, knows it, everybody. But, after every crash of
civilization there has been chaos,—and by the way, notice
with what love and affection he speaks of the Greeks,—he
speaks about Plato and the artists, and the tragedians and
all in the same loving way. Yet, how do we know about
them? There is some progress, obviously. He tells us we
have not their equals. Why should we want equals? We
have **them** today just as truly as if they were in our midst.
Just as truly.

Well, I am willing to admit all the dreadfulness of the
present situation. I would go him better, but I believe that
things ahead have hope. Notice that while conditions in our
civilization are bad, and while much of that civilization has
crashed, and much of what we were proud of, is gone, and
gone forever, yet we have made some gains in attitude. I
did not intend to back up old arguments; I read that debate
between Kennedy and Darrow on much the same subject
as we are discussing, and I supposed that most of you here
had. I did not believe Mr. Darrow would come before you
with that old stuff over again, and yet almost all of what he
said to you during the actual forty minutes was that same
stuff. I meant to avoid absolutely what was said by Mr.
Darrow and Mr. Kennedy in that old debate, but I will come
back to this much. Look at that culture of which he is so
fond in Greece; what proportion in Greece were slaves?
You tell men that there is such a thing as different forms of
slavery. I admit it. But the actual matter of human slavery
is a thing that it almost gone, and in civilization it is gone.
There may be other things analogous to it that are bad, but
they will go just as slavery has gone!

We have improved in independence. Oh, sure, yes, I am
so thankful that Mr. Darrow did not indulge in that maudlin
praise which I rather expected he would indulge in in regard
to the happy life of the savage and the barbarian. I will not
refer to that African on the banks of the Yang-tse Kiang
whose ideal situation he only dimly painted before you, because he did not want to bring me out in regard to savages,
you know. Well, he did not say much about the ideal situation of the savage and of the barbarian, because it would be

painful to hear him talk of a thing of which he actually knew nothing. It would be painful. He omitted that. But, notice, in savagery this thing is true; everybody does just what everybody else does; and if anybody does anything different from what everybody else does, he pays the penalty. And, I have often wondered how quickly Mr. Darrow would have found his end, if he had lived in savagery—because in savagery, at the first tendency to show independence in life, thought or action, off with his head, tear him to pieces, and throw his scattered remains to those alligators that he talks so affectionately of, out there on the banks, the sand-banks of the river!

Well, now, that is all right, but you know, really, Mr. Darrow would not have lasted long in savagery. No, it is civilization, with all its faults which tolerates him. By the way, he did not quite define it as I did. He made it a more artificial thing than I did. I merely said it was the adjustment of the individual to live in crowds. That is what it is. And in civilization, individuals of different kinds have different opinions, different ideals, different ideas that they may express with a fair degree of safety. It is only in civilization when it comes to the point, that there is social independence. In this frightful crisis of the present moment, have we civilization? No; because in civilization men, women and children, stand a better chance of speaking frankly, and fully and freely than in any other state of culture. And, in every true civilization, toward which I hope we look forward, independence is the rule!

Then, there is another attitude of mind, that is interesting, which is the matter of brotherhood. It does not look like brotherhood now on the battlefields of Europe. It does not look much like brotherhood right here among us. No. I admit all that, but I know that the brotherhood of man is a doctrine that has gained ground, and is gaining ground with every generation that passes, and will gain ground until there is a general feeling of brotherhood. And, the time is coming as quickly and as fast as you play your part and show yourself the brother of the man with whom you come in contact.

Diversity of gifts! Yes, diversity of gifts. I am not anxious that every man should be an anthropologist. I do not care a cent if there are lawyers in the world, even. I am perfectly willing to have lawyers in the world, especially when they are ready to devote their talents to worthy causes. I welcome even lawyers, and lecturers on astronomy and socialism, and every kind of thing. Why yes; we want diversity: we want diversity of thoughts.

You know this is the first time I ever heard Mr. Darrow really talk in public. I have conversed with him personally;

I have met him as a teacher meets a student; but I have never had the pleasure of hearing Mr. Darrow in public before. I have been told so many things about him. I have been told about his brilliant oratory; I have heard about his familiar manner, about his ingratiating mode of dealing with his audience; that he carries them right in his hand. You can imagine with what fear and terror I looked forward to this meeting. But, now, what I want to say about Mr. Darrow is this: They had always told me that he was blackly pessimistic, and you know I have been looking this afternoon for the pessimism. There is some of it there; some pessimism, but not so much; not so much. They tell me he presides at dinners to the memory of Tom Paine, and I understand he is an admirer of Walt Whitman. Isn't that a curious aggregation for a pessimist? Yes, for a pessimist who loves Tom Paine and Walt Whitman. Birds of a feather flock together. Think of the deep pessimism of Walt Whitman and Tom Paine! No, they were people who believed in men; they were people who believed in brotherhood; they were people who believed in a hope of bright sun-rise; something in the future; progress, advancement. Don't tell me that a man is densely pessimistic who presides over dinners for Tom Paine!

After all, you know, we might be worse; we might be worse. I very rarely quote people. Very rarely a man says a thing as well as I think I can say it myself. But here I want to quote a passage from a man, an Assyrian, Ribbany, who says:

"Furthermore, America has been making the experiment of racial amalgamation on the vastest scale the world has yet known, and with great success. Never since the world began did the children of so many races assemble under one flag to work out the problem of individual and national destiny as **free men** as are assembled in America today. The ancient empires—Persia, Babylon, Assyria, Egypt, Greece, Rome—every one of them ruled many nations and races, but they ruled those people with a rod of iron and did not educate them for citizenship and treat them as equals. This country has proven to the world that the sons and daughters of many different races and the adherents of many different creeds, millions in number, could live together peaceably as free citizens of one commonwealth, and have one supreme national ideal."

Something to it?

It is not all we wish it was, no, and it has the earmarks of a mad-house for the moment, but there is something to it; there is something to it in the fact that you and I hope, and confidently look forward to in the future. Yes, toward which we aim.

I want to read you three quotations. They are quotations from different kinds of people. They are all from people who have been speaking on this question of what lies ahead, what is in the future. One of them is Edward Carpenter. Now, of course, you know more about Edward Carpenter than I do. I have not read so very much of that writer, but he is interesting. I do not always follow him, but let us see what he says. He has been talking about civilization. He has been tracing it backwards; he has been telling how it is a disease; he has been wondering whether it is necessarily fatal, and absolutely sure to kill, or whether there is some hope for the future; and toward the end of his discourse, he says:

"Possibly some day we shall again build our houses or dwelling places so simple and elemental in character, that they will fit in the nooks of the hills or along the banks of the streams, or by the edges of the woods, without disturbing the harmony of the landscape or the songs of the birds. Then the great temples, beautiful on every height, or by the shores of the rivers and the lakes, will be the storehouses of all precious and lovely things. There men, women and children will come to share in the great and wonderful common life, the gardens around will be sacred to the unharmed and welcome animals; there all store and all facilities of books and music and art for everyone, there a meeting place for social life and intercourse, there dances and games, and feasts. Every village, every little settlement will have such hall or halls. No need for private accumulations. Gladly will each man, and more gladly still, each woman, take his or her treasures, except what are immediately or necessarily in use, to the common centre, where their value will be increased a hundred and a thousand fold by the greater number of those who can enjoy them, and where far more perfectly and with far less evil they can be tended than if scattered abroad in private hands. At one stroke half the labor and all the anxiety of domestic caretaking will be annihilated. The private dwelling places, no longer costly and labyrinthine in proportion to the value and number of the treasures they contain, will need no longer to have doors and windows jealously closed against fellow-man or mother Nature. The sun and air will have access to them, the indwellers will have unfettered egress. Neither man nor woman will be tied in slavery to the lodge which they inhabit; and in becoming once more a part of Nature, the human habitation will at length cease to be what it is now for, at least, half the human race—a prison."

Of course, I consider that rather fantastic. It is very, very beautiful; it is an ideal which one would gladly see achieved. But, to me it sounds rather fantastic. Read it as the hope of aspiration, the ideal of a man who recognizes as fully as any speaker in this room today can do, the evil and inherent dangers of civilization. And, yet he looked forward; Edward Carpenter, to some escape, to a future.

My second quotation is a very different class of matter. It is from one of the great geologists of the world. Of course, a geologist is a man whom you would hardly expect to have an opinion regarding the future. A great geologist, of course, primarily, is interested in the past. But, let me read:

From Text Book of College Geology, by Dr. Thomas C. Chamberlain and Dr. Rollin D. Salisbury, pages 943-4:

"A Psychozoic era, as long as the Cenozoic or the Paleozoic, or an eon as long as the cosmic and the biotic ones, may quite as well be predicted as anything less. The forecast is at best speculative, but an optimistic outlook seems more likely to prove true than a pessimistic one. An immeasurably higher evolution than that now reached, with attainments beyond present comprehension, is a reasonable hope.

"The forecast of an eon of intellectual and spiritual development comparable in magnitude to the prolonged physical and biotic evolutions, lends to the total view of earth-history great moral satisfaction, and the thought that individual contributions to the higher-welfare of the race may realize their fullest fruits by continued influence through scarcely limited ages, gives value to life and inspiration to personal endeavor."

The quotation shows what a thoughtful geologist, looking back upon the long, long past, and looking forward to a long, long, future, thinks he may reasonably hope for from this world.

The third quotation is a very recent one, from an address delivered in this city in the past month, by Roger W. Babson, at the banquet of the Chicago Association of Credit Men, Hotel La Salle, January 30, 1920. He spoke as follows, and he was quoting Mr. Edison, and it is because of Mr. Edison's remark that it seems to me the quotation has some interest:

"I was visiting Mr. Edison some two years ago and asked him what he thought would be the greatest invention of the next generation. He shook his shaggy head and said: 'Well, Babson, I have often thought about that myself. I doubt a good deal if it will be along mechanical lines. You will be surprised to hear me say this, but I sort of feel that it will be along psychological or spiritual lines. I sort of feel that somebody, some time, is going to invent something which will get people to have the right point of view toward life, and that is what America is waiting for today, and only that will solve her problems and reduce the cost of living."

Now notice, I do not consider Edward Carpenter a final authority. No. I do not consider Thomas C. Chamberlain an absolute authority in regard to a psychozoic era lying ahead. I do not consider Thomas Edison the last word in regard to the future, no. But, it is rather interesting to find three men, thoughtful men, sensible men, men of position, men of standing, whose ideas have some weight and value, take such views in a moment of crisis like this. Yes, it is something that Edward Carpenter, Thomas C. Chamberlain and Thomas Edison get together on common ground, in looking forward with hope to the future, instead of seeing nothing but blackness ahead. That I think is worth calling attention to and worth emphasizing.

Now, let me return to my broken discussion, I had spoken about the great war and the frightful chaos that has followed after the war, the suffering, the uncertainty, the hideous condition in the world today. And, what of the future is there ahead? I believe there is hope, yes, or I would not stand here and say so. It seems to me there is hope for the future. I used to ask the question, when I told my young people that this crash was coming,—and they will bear me out that I have told them so for twenty years—they will bear me out that for twenty years I have told them that our civilization was just as certain to fall when its hour came as any civilization that ever existed. Well, the hour came, the civilization has fallen. We are only just beginning to realize something as to the significance and actuality of the wreck.

Well, what about the future? Is there any chance or hope? I used to say to my young people, "Is there somewhere a young race, a people that has been living sheltered, who can seize the torch and carry it on?" I really used to feel that the earth had been made so small, that it had been so compressed, that in this period of material development it had been so contracted, that there really was no chance of any nation or any people seizing that falling torch. I had once hoped that it would be Japan; but Japan has been so much infected, so much imbued with western ideals, it has lost so much of what was fine, and strong and genuine in it, that I look for little hope so far as world leadership is concerned, so far as that torch is concerned, from Japan alone. I once thought there was some hope in China. I now doubt whether China will seize the falling torch and carry it along.

What then is the hope, or is there none? I believe there is hope, but I look for it in a new direction. While I think the world today is so small that there is no single mass of mankind who can seize the torch of civilization and carry it on to higher things, I still believe there is hope. According to the old maxim, "er oriente lux"—I look to the east for light. I believe there is a sun-rise coming, and I believe the hope for to-morrow lies in just the place where thirty years ago I told people the great work of the world lay.

There are two nations on whom the future rests. We may be a mad-house. I hope we recover. I hope we will improve. I hope we will come back to sanity. I hope we will stand for the finest things in our past. But even if we do, the world's salvation will not come from the United States. No. I believe that the two great nations of the world in the coming hundred years will be one great nation of white people and one great nation of yellow. I believe that in Russia—poor Russia, bleeding Russia, and in China, down-trodden China, the greatest aggregation of yellow people in the world, the future world hope lies, and it cannot come from one nor from the other. Too long civilization has been seized and carried by one people, one nation. Now, it must be Russia and China, united with the best from both, that shall carry on the movement.

Do not misunderstand me. I am not pleading now a conquest of Russia by China nor a conquest of China by Russia, but I hope that Russia has yet enough foundation, enough of strong vigor, enough of those things which are best in the white race to have life to live; and I hope that China retains out of the ancient past, that fundamental altruism which, added to what Russia has, will make a union based on principles higher and finer than any we have ever seen. With the union of the best from the old domestic civilization of Asia, and the best from the later political civilization of Europe, I hope in this future, through the impregnation of the one set of ideals by the other, to see something finer, better, stronger, more widespread, world-embracing, such as the world has never seen. **Ex oriente lux.** In China and in Russia, there are the ideals which united mean liberty, success, advancement, opportunity for each man to live his best and noblest life.

It seems to me that these men are not mistaken; that there is a future; that the old world has not finished; that we may look forward to a civilization, truer, better, more honest, more genuine, than the world has ever seen!

The Chairman: Mr. Darrow.

Mr. Darrow: My friend's faith in the world getting anywhere has come down to a hope. Well, that is all right. To me "hope" sounds so much like "dope," that I never could see much in it. I don't object to a man hoping. I hope sometimes too, when I know there is nothing in it. That is one thing that makes me hope. All of this is in the province of faith. I knew I should have had a religious man to oppose me on this question. This whole thing is in the realm of faith. I don't know what may come. I could not prove that there are not fairies. Perhaps there are. I have hope. But, if a man tells me there are fairies, it is up to him to show me the fairy. I know the fairy tales.

I would not call Edward Carpenter a scientist; neither does my friend. He gives us a pretty picture. What of it? I would not call the geologist a student of sociology. He understands geology. He did not find proof of his theories in the rocks. Edison has been saying some things, and he has a good deal of idealism in him. Why are the words of Edison taken up by Babson, whose business is to get out a paper dealing with the stock market? I will tell you why. Edison has intellect enough to know, and I fancy Babson has intellect enough to know, that all of this thing that we call civilization today, is a bubble; it is nothing; it is a fleeting show; it does not satisfy an intellectual man, a man of vision and dream, and therefore he paints these pictures and these dreams. Edison says sometime we will turn to spiritual things? Why? Because he knows that the things he has given to the world have done little to make the world happier or better; because he sees this mad race for wealth and he knows it means nothing. He has a dream that some time we will turn to spiritual things. Well, of course, he does not say what "spiritual" things, any more than Mary Baker G. Eddy does. What does he mean by "spiritual" things? The word really has no scientific meaning.

Man is just the way he is, whether he is as completely fixed as the ant and the bee,—which perhaps he is not—he is practically fixed; he is a part of nature, a specific part, with a definite origin, with definite capacities; has accomplished definite

things, and failed in definite things, and there is no room that
I can see, in life or experience or logic or science to say he can
ever to differently in the future from what he has done in the
past.

My friend here has dreams. Dreams are good. The only
trouble with them is that you awaken. I have dreams. I often
purposely go to sleep in the morning and sleep an hour or two
longer because I know what it is when I am awake, and I don't
know when I am dreaming. I am satisfied to let him and Walt
Whitman and all the rest of them dream, and to a certain extent I sympathize with them. But why should he say that
Russia and China are to do different things for the human race
than have been done in all the ages that have gone before?

Now, I have a deep profound sympathy for Russia in her
present experiment, and I hope she will succeed! Suppose
she does or does not, what has that to do with the question
of what the human race has accomplished or what the human race can do; and that its future as a future will be different from its past. Life is an ever ebbing and flowing, a
coming and going—what else?

There is only one reason I can see why Russia should take
up the torch in Europe, and that is that Russia is the newest—
in a sense, of the peoples of the world; a primitive nation,
closer to nature, closer to life, and she might do something
new; but. with the knowledge of the past, is there any reason
to think that even if she did that she will not go the course of
Persia and Egypt and Rome and Greece, and the course that
Great Britain will one day go, and that the United States will
one day go? Is the law of birth and growth and decay any
different with nations than it is with individuals? Will it be
any different in the future than it has been in the past? I fail
to see a scrap of evidence that it will be any different in the
future than it has been in the past.

Perhaps China may some day awaken from her long slum-
ber, and I don't know what she will do when she has been
awakened. China today has solved the problem of the greatest mass of people getting along with each other better than
any other nation in the world. She is more densely populated
than any of the rest, and she seems to have learned this great
law of accommodating each to all better than any other nation
in the world. If she becomes civilized, she will probably forget it and go the way of the rest!

Now, I don't despair. I haven't anything to despair of.
I see the game as the game has been played since the world
began, as far as I can see the record, and it is the game of the
child, born full of hope, reaching middle age, full of ambi-
tion, doing his work, finally reaching the period of decay and

dying, getting through with it; it has been the life of the individual, it has been the life of the race, it has been the life of each separate nation of the race. What is there in life, or experience or science to show that it will be any different in time to come?

Has my friend given you one single fact in anthropology, that he is so familiar with, or in science, that he is so familiar with, to show that there is anything but the law of life and death? Ebb and flow—everlasting change—in and out— that makes up human life?

Are the emotions of men today any different than they ever were? Voltaire, who perhaps did more for the improvement of the human race than most any intellect the world has ever know—Voltaire, the great iconoclast, fought against the very intolerance that is rife all over the world today. He raised his voice in the face of prison and death for the right of men to live, to express their opinion as they would. We thought it had been established in the world, and lo and behold, almost as if by magic, the right is gone, and all the fierce hatred and bitterness of the past has come in its place. Why is it that great masses of men and women, who have had years of training and experience, and a large degree of freedom can be caught by such a fool phrase as "a hundred per cent American?" Why is it that we can forget all our traditions and send thousands of poor, working people, out of our country, in a mad passion, and frenzy, at the command of a few? Why is it that a boy could be turned out of a public school in Chicago because he did not see fit to salute a flag, whether he believed in the flag or not? Why is it that tolerance and common intelligence can never long rule the brains of man? Men are moved by catch words, by feelings, by emotions, and they do all the barbarous things today that they did when the human race was young.

Speaking of Greece. True, she had slaves. But, take the slaves with them, and the whole mass of the population probably averaged much higher intellectually there than it does in America today. We have had chattle slaves, literally in this country, sixty years ago, and we thought nothing about it. It is a matter of custom and habit mainly. But, you may go back to the old Grecians and even farther back than that, and there were still those men who did not believe in slavery; still those men who had the same dreams the Professor has, the same dreams that Edward Carpenter has, the same dreams that all dreamers have. The truth is that it is the abnormal men who have them; the men who are not like his fellow-man. The men with deseased brains. But, life is continually preserved by the medium person. If you want a presidential candidate, get a common place man, a man who has never expressed any radical opinion on anything, the great mass is for him. You will find it true everywhere. It is the great, common place that has ruled the world. Phrases; catch words, it is not the philosophers or the dreamers. It is these men. And when they are touched by a great feeling, great emotion, good or bad, they are like the wolves that hunt in packs, and all reason falls from them.

Has the Professor shown that we are happier? That we are better? He tells us we know more of brotherhood. Where does he get it? We trace a dream of brotherhood in all the peoples of the earth. I suppose he had in mind the negroes down on the south side, where the white men are organizing themselves, the good, respectable ones, into bombing committees to destroy their homes. Has our feeling changed? Almost none, if any; possibly some; railroads and better communication have done something to draw peoples together; the man who is densely ignorant is the person who is outside the stream of life.

But, this is only one phase of life, and we are everlastingly reverting to the common type; the common type, which I say cannot possibly be changed; you can make nothing out of a man but a man, that is all. He is susceptible to a certain development, a certain growth, and no more; and I submit that there is nothing in the history of the world or the experience of life to show that this statement is not true.

Now, I really ought to discuss this question with a man who seriously has faith that this world is getting better. With a man who can stand on a platform and say today is perfect, look what we have. Instead of a man who says, "Well, it is true, this world is a mad house, it is true civilization is breaking down, and he goes me one better and says it will be destroyed. All right; it is true that everything has failed in the past; that nations have risen and died, but I have a dream that some time it will be better."

Well, I don't know what he takes, exactly. If I did, I would be glad to get some of it. I hope it will be better, but I don't hope it in the sense of expecting it. I don't expect it. I can see nothing in man to make him intrinsically different from what he has always been, any more than I can see anything in an ape to make the ape intrinsically different from what he was; or anything in an ant to make him any more than the ant has been.

I can see nothing from which to prophecy for the future, except the past. And, in the whole scheme of the universe, I can see no law that teaches me that there is any beneficient power working to make the world better in the future than it has been in the past. You believe it will be better. Let me suggest that if we are to believe it, it implies one of two or three things: Either that there is a Supreme Being, who holds in his hands the destinies not only of all the peoples, but of all life on the earth; but it also implies that that Supreme Being is good; and there is no evidence in science for either statement.

If not that, it implies that there is a certain physical law which we may call the law of evolution, and that this law is beneficient, and it cannot be beneficient unless some beneficient power planned it.

He seems to take exception to my idea of Nature. Nature, red with tooth and claw. Well, the stories about the goodness of Nature are simply myths and lullabye tales. Nature is not necessarily good or bad. She is simply all-powerful. She brings some happiness to many; she likewise brings misery to all. She will cause the joys of friendship to turn to pain and grief at the loss of friends. No one can point at Nature, blind, cruel, unpitying and say there is anything good in Her. Perhaps there is nothing bad in Her, but certainly nothing beneficient. And, as to man, he is helpless in her hands. In her blindness, she has developed him as he is. Just as she has developed everything else as it is. His limitations are fixed. The laws of his being are exact and you have no right to blame him or praise him. He cannot make it better excepting here and there, and now and then, when this inspiration is upon him, or that is upon him.

It is the nature of life to change, move, out and in, and up and down, and forward and backward, restless, forever, with no beginning and no end; a ship on the sea, tossed by every wave and by every wind; a ship headed for no port and no harbor, with no rudder, no compass, no pilot; simply floating for a time, then lost in the waves.

This is life, and I submit, it is all that science can tell us of life.

The Chairman: Before Professor Starr closes his debate, I think I should tell you that we have the promise of one more Darrow-Starr Debate before the season closes, on the question: Is Life Worth Living?

Professor Starr: Now, I shall not take the fifteen minutes that have been offered to me; I shall not take ten, I shall not take five. It is not necessary so far as any new argument is concerned. I only want to say two things in regard to what has been said since I spoke; the first one is to still voice my surprise at the presentation, after the old-world, anthropomorphisation-style, of nature. I really am more pained and surprised now than I was before.

I want to say just one word with regard to Russia and China. Why have I some hope in regard to Russia and China? Look at the present conditions in Russia. We there have the best of what is vital and promising in the white race and white blood; in China we have the fundamental idea that has kept China a nation and a crowded one for four thousand years. Talk about her being civilized! She was civilized before the birth of Christ. Talk about China as a nation! She has outlived most of the nations of history. And why? Because, the fundamental idea underlying China's society and China's policies is altruism. In China the individual counts for nothing; the mass counts for everything. That does not mean that the individual may not be an individual. It does not mean that he may not think for himself, speak for himself, act for himself; but it means that in the crisis he should sacrifice himself for all.

Now, in the combination of those two ideas, we have something the past has never shown. For the development of the world, China and Russia are side by side. I believe something is coming of that contact.

Talk about dreams. Why, I don't even dream when I go to sleep. Talk about spirits. You don't hear me regret the loss of any spirits, do you? No?

No, my bitterest enemy does not talk about my dreaming. No, indeed. I look forward with hope; yes. Notice, Mr. Darrow said that my hope came down out of faith. Why, no, it has nothing to do with faith; but if it had relation to faith, it could come up from faith. Hope does not come down from anything; hope comes up from everything. And, I tell you if we have in us some capacity; if we have in us some ability of development and range, and we have (even Mr. Darrow assumed it, he merely recognized limits on either side) ground for hope. The trouble is that we do not come up to the upper limit—and I venture to say there was never a time in the world's history when more people might come up to the upper limit than among us. Let us then look forward, with hope to the future. I do not ask that you be super-men. I know nothing about super-men. I do not wish super-men. What I want is real men. I want men who do come up to the possibilities of their own make-up. If every man does that, there is no question about whether we are advancing, because that thing never has been yet, and it has come nearer to happening within the past two hundred years than it ever did in the history of the world before. In that possibility, let all of us surpass our past, realizing that we have a better opportunity in the present and future than in the past, let us have hope, which is no dream.

CPSIA information can be obtained
at www.ICGtesting.com
Printed in the USA
BVHW050212230522
637788BV00006B/185